DIY

RV

Repair

by

Billy J Riggs

ISBN: 97983889229075

Printed in the United States of
America

First printing 2023

Table of Contents

ABOUT THE AUTHOR

Bill has had a broad 40-year career working in the construction and remodeling trades. This has provided him with an extensive background in mechanical, plumbing, and electrical systems as well as interior remodeling best practices. Since 2020, he's been inspecting, remodeling, and repairing all types of RVs. In 2023, he added RV transport/delivery and a mobile repair service. This allowed him to finally make the leap from building construction and repair to a full time RV inspection company. Since Bill enjoys all things RV, so the business is aptly named:

https://www.associatedrvservices.com

INTRODUCTION

Whether you RV full-time, part-time, or sometimes, the RV lifestyle includes many benefits one might not otherwise experience. One of the biggest benefits of the RV lifestyle is the freedom and flexibility it offers. RVers can travel wherever they want, whenever they want, without being tied down by a fixed itinerary or schedule. RV travel can also be an affordable way to explore new places, as it eliminates the need for expensive flights, hotels, and restaurants. One of my favorites is that RVs offer all the comforts of home, including a bed, kitchen, bathroom, and living space. This allows RVers to travel in comfort and convenience, without sacrificing the comforts of home.

RVers can immerse themselves in nature and experience the great outdoors in a way that is not possible with other types of travel. RVs allow you to camp in scenic locations and explore national parks, forests, and other natural wonders.

The RV community is known for being friendly, welcoming, and supportive. People often form lasting friendships with other travelers they meet on the road. The RV lifestyle is full of adventure and excitement, as RVers can explore new places, try new things, and have new experiences every day. Some of those experiences are not positive though. RVs shake, rattle, and roll down highways at speeds up to 70 mph. (Consider that a tropical storm is considered a hurricane when its wind speeds reach 74 mph.) As a result, things on an RV break – and often.

During covid, demand was so high for RVs that the units are completely built in just four days. While some manufacturers have rigorous quality control checks, others aren't as diligent. Dealers often give the RVs a cursory review when they arrive on the lots just to make sure they are ready for display. Even if the post-sale repairs are covered by warranty, it can often take months to get the RV back from the service department. Yet, buyers must continue to make monthly payments and, of course, don't get to enjoy using the RV.

Keep Your Money!

The average annual amount spent on RV repairs can vary widely depending on the age and condition of the RV, as well as the type and frequency of maintenance and repairs performed. According to a survey conducted by RVIA (Recreational Vehicle Industry Association) in 2021, the average annual maintenance and repair cost for a new RV is approximately $1,200 per year. For a used RV, the average annual maintenance and repair cost is approximately $1,800 per year. However, these are just averages, and individual experiences can vary greatly depending on factors such as the specific RV model, how frequently it is used, and how well it is maintained. Additionally, unexpected repairs or major maintenance needs can significantly increase these costs. RV owners need to be able to troubleshoot and do their own repairs for several reasons. Here are some of the main reasons:

Cost savings: Repairing an RV can be expensive, and many RV owners could save money by doing their own repairs. By learning how to troubleshoot and fix common issues, RV owners can avoid costly repair bills and keep their RVs in good working order.

Convenience: When traveling in an RV, it's not always easy to find a repair shop or mechanic when something goes wrong. Being able to troubleshoot and do your own repairs can help you quickly get your RV back on the road and avoid long delays or interruptions in your trip.

Safety: Proper maintenance and repairs are essential for ensuring the safety of the vehicle and its passengers. RV owners who know how to troubleshoot and repair their own vehicles can ensure that their RVs are in good working order and minimize the risk of accidents or breakdowns.

Empowerment: Learning how to troubleshoot and do your own repairs can be empowering and give RV owners a sense of control over their vehicle. It can also be a fun and rewarding hobby for those who enjoy working on vehicles and learning new skills. Overall, being able to troubleshoot and do your own repairs is an important skill for RV owners. It can help save downtime, money, increase convenience, improve safety, and provide a sense of empowerment and satisfaction.

Understanding the Difference Between RV Maintenance Items and Warranty Work

RV maintenance items and warranty work are two different types of services related to maintaining and repairing an RV. RV maintenance items refer to routine maintenance tasks that are required to keep an RV running smoothly and prevent breakdowns. These can include things like oil changes, tire rotations, battery maintenance, regularly examining the roof and repairing the sealant defects around plumbing penetrations and roof vents, and other regular maintenance tasks. Maintenance items are typically the responsibility of the RV owner, and the cost of maintenance is not covered by the RV manufacturer's warranty.

On the other hand, warranty work is repair work that is covered by the manufacturer's warranty. This includes repairs or replacements of components that fail due to defects in materials or workmanship. Warranty work is typically performed by authorized service centers and is covered by the manufacturer for a specified period of time. It is important for RV owners to understand the difference between maintenance items and warranty work, as proper maintenance can help prevent warranty claims and ensure that the RV runs smoothly throughout its life. Additionally, RV owners should carefully review the terms and conditions of their manufacturer's warranty to understand what is and is not covered under the warranty.

DISCLAIMER OF RESPONSIBILITY

"The information contained in this RV repair guide is for educational purposes only and is provided 'as is' without warranty of any kind, either express or implied. The author and publisher of this guide disclaim any liability for any damage or injuries arising from the use of this guide. The user of this guide assumes all responsibility for any repairs or modifications made to their RV based on the information provided in this guide. Always follow manufacturer's instructions and seek professional assistance if you are not confident in your ability to perform a repair or modification."

This disclaimer serves as a warning to the reader that the guide is not a substitute for professional advice or expertise, and that the user assumes all risks associated with any repairs or modifications made to their RV. It also encourages users to seek professional assistance if they are not confident in their ability to perform a repair or modification and reminds them to always follow manufacturer's instructions.

EVEN LUXURY RVs HAVE ISSUES

RVs require regular maintenance to stay in good working condition. Here are some of the most common RV repairs that RV owners may encounter:

Electrical issues: Problems with the RV's electrical system are common. This may include issues with the battery, wiring, or fuses. Common symptoms of electrical issues may include lights that won't turn on, appliances that won't work, or other electrical components that malfunction.

Plumbing problems: Issues with the RV's plumbing system are also common. This may include leaky pipes, clogged drains, or problems with the RV's water pump. Symptoms may include low water pressure, leaks, or unpleasant odors venting into the living space of your RV.

Roof damage: RV roofs can become damaged from exposure to the elements and when passing by or under trees. This may include cracks, leaks, or punctures. Symptoms of roof damage may include water stains or dampness inside the RV and delamination of the roof membrane.

Tire issues: RV tires can wear out quickly and may need to be replaced more frequently than car tires. Common tire issues may include flat tires, blowouts, or uneven wear.

HVAC problems: The RV's heating, ventilation, and air conditioning (HVAC) system may also experience problems. Common issues may include malfunctioning thermostats, clogged filters, or issues with the RV's air conditioning compressor.

Slide-out problems: Many RVs have slide-outs, which can become misaligned, stuck or just malfunction. Symptoms of slide-out problems may include difficulty extending or retracting the slide-out, or the slide-out becoming stuck in the wrong position.

TOOLS RV OWNERS SHOULD OWN AND KNOW HOW TO USE

Generally speaking, regular maintenance and inspections can help prevent many common RV repairs. However, RV owners should be prepared and equipped to troubleshoot and address common issues to keep their RVs in good working condition. There are several tools that RV owners should have on hand and be familiar with to help with maintenance and repairs while on the road. Here are some examples:

Basic hand tools: A set of basic hand tools, including screwdrivers, pliers, wrenches, hammer, cordless drill, and socket sets, can be very useful for general repairs and maintenance. These make great gift ideas for birthdays, anniversaries, Mother's or Father's Day, Christmas, etc.

Multimeter: A multimeter is a tool that can measure electrical current, voltage, and resistance. It can be helpful in diagnosing electrical problems and ensuring that the RV's electrical systems are functioning properly.

Tire pressure gauge: Maintaining proper tire pressure is important for safety and fuel efficiency. A tire pressure gauge allows RV owners to check the tire pressure and ensure that it is at the manufacturer's recommended inflation level quickly and easily.

Leveling blocks: Leveling blocks can be used to level the RV and prevent it from rocking or shaking while parked. This can improve comfort and prevent damage to the RV's leveling, plumbing, and propane refrigeration systems.

Torque wrench: A torque wrench is a tool used to tighten bolts to a specific level of tightness. This is important for maintaining proper tension on critical components like wheel lugs and engine bolts.

Sewer hose and fittings: RV owners should have a sewer hose and fittings for dumping waste from the RV's holding tanks.

Emergency kit: An emergency kit should include items like a first-aid kit, flashlight, LED flares/hazard lights, batteries, water, and non-perishable food. This can be important in case of unexpected breakdowns or emergencies.

RV owners should also be familiar with how to use these tools and perform basic maintenance tasks, as well as knowing when to seek professional help for more complicated repairs.

PRIMARY SYSTEMS IN AN RV

An RV (recreational vehicle) typically has several primary systems that allow it to function as a self-contained living space. These systems may vary depending on the type and size of the RV, but some common primary systems include:

Electrical System: This system provides power to the RV's appliances, lights, and other electrical devices. It typically includes a battery or set of batteries, an inverter, and a converter to switch between AC and DC power.

Plumbing System: This system provides water for the RV's sink, shower, and toilet, as well as a way to remove wastewater. It typically includes a freshwater tank, a gray water tank, and a black water tank.

Propane System: This system provides fuel for the RV's stove, oven, and other appliances that use propane. It typically includes a propane tank and a regulator.

Heating and Cooling System: This system provides temperature control for the RV, keeping it comfortable in hot or cold weather. It may include a furnace, air conditioner, or both.

Chassis System: This includes the engine, transmission, suspension, and other components that allow the RV to move on the road.

Safety System: This includes features such as smoke detectors, carbon monoxide detectors, fire extinguishers, and emergency exits to ensure the safety of the RV occupants.

COMMON RV ELECTRICAL ISSUES

Before we discuss the steps to troubleshoot common RV electrical issues, I want to address some common concerns some people have regarding working around electricity. First, there is nothing wrong with have a healthy respect for electricity. As a seasoned master electrician, I can assure you that overcoming a fear of electricity can be challenging, but it is possible with the right approach. Here are some steps that may help:

Educate yourself: Learn about electricity, how it works, and the safety measures you can take to protect yourself. This can help you understand the risks and reduce anxiety.

Start small: Begin with small electrical tasks, such as changing a light bulb or plugging in an appliance. This can help you build confidence and feel more comfortable working with electricity.

Take a course or workshop: Consider taking a course or workshop on electrical safety or basic electrical skills. This can provide hands-on experience and expert guidance.

Practice safety measures: Always practice safety measures when working with electricity, such as wearing protective gear and turning off power sources before working on electrical components.

Seek support: If your fear of electricity is interfering with your daily life or causing significant anxiety, consider seeking support from a mental health professional or support group.

Remember that overcoming a fear of electricity takes time and patience. Take it one step at a time and seek help if you need it. With practice and education, you can develop the skills and confidence to safely work with electricity.

How Electricity Works

Electricity is the flow of electrons through a conductor, such as a wire. Electrons are negatively charged particles that orbit around the positively charged nucleus of an atom. Normally, electrons are tightly bound to their atoms and do not move around freely. However, when an external force is applied to the atoms, such as a difference in electrical potential, some of the electrons can be "knocked" free from their atoms and become free to move. This creates a flow of electrons through the conductor, known as an electric current.

The strength of electrical current is measured in amperes, or amps. The rate at which electric charge flows through a conductor is measured in volts, or voltage. The resistance to the flow of electric current in a conductor is measured in ohms.

Electricity can be generated in various ways, including through the movement of magnets inside a wire coil (known as electromagnetic induction), chemical reactions in batteries, or by harnessing the energy of falling water in hydroelectric power plants.

Electricity is used in many applications, such as powering appliances and lighting, operating electronic devices, and providing energy for transportation. However, it is important to handle electricity safely, as it can be dangerous if one gets distracted.

Why You Should Own a Multimeter

A multimeter is a useful tool for troubleshooting electrical issues. Here are some steps to use a multimeter to troubleshoot electrical issues:

Set the multimeter: Set the multimeter to the appropriate function for the measurement you want to take. For example, if you want to measure voltage, set the multimeter to the AC or DC voltage function.

Connect the probes: Connect the probes to the appropriate terminals. For example, if you want to measure voltage, connect the red probe to the positive (+) terminal and the black probe to the negative (-) terminal.

Test the circuit: Touch the probes to the circuit you want to test. For example, if you want to test a battery, touch the probes to the positive and negative terminals of the battery.

Read the display: Read the measurement on the multimeter display. For example, if you are measuring voltage, the display will show the voltage reading.

Interpret the results: Interpret the results to diagnose the problem. For example, if the voltage reading is low, the problem may be a low battery or a faulty power source.

Repeat as necessary: Repeat the steps as necessary to test different circuits or components.

It's important to note that when using a multimeter, always follow the manufacturer's instructions and safety guidelines. Never touch the probes to live electrical components or circuits, as this can be dangerous or even deadly. Always wear appropriate protective equipment, such as gloves and safety glasses, when working with electrical components. Let's get started.

Step-by-Step RV Electrical Testing Protocol:

RVs typically have three electrical systems; chassis lighting, dc (house battery) power, and ac power (when plugged into shore power). Know where your fuse box is and how to troubleshoot basic electrical issues.

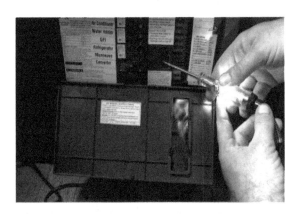

Check the power source: Make sure the RV is properly connected to a power source, such as a generator or shore power. Check the circuit breaker and fuses to ensure they are not tripped or blown.

Check the battery: If the RV is not connected to a power source, check the battery. Make sure it is charged and in good working condition. If the battery is low, recharge it using a battery charger or a generator.

Check the wiring: Check the wiring in the RV for any loose, damaged or corroded connections.

Use a multimeter to check for continuity and voltage.

Check the appliances: If only some appliances or outlets are not working, check those specific appliances. Make sure they are properly plugged in and that their circuits are not tripped. If an appliance is not working properly, it may be faulty and need to be repaired or replaced.

Check the inverter: If the RV has an inverter, check it to ensure it is working properly. Use a multimeter to test the voltage output.

Check the converter: If the RV is connected to a power source but the battery is not charging, check the converter. Use a multimeter to test the voltage output.

Check the ground fault circuit interrupter (GFCI): If outlets or appliances are not working, check the GFCI. Reset it if it has tripped.

By following these steps, RV owners can diagnose and fix many common electrical issues. However, if these steps do not solve the problem, it may be necessary to seek professional help from a qualified RV technician.

RV PLUMBING SYSTEM ISSUES

RV plumbing systems can experience a variety of problems, but some of the most common ones include:

Leaks: Leaks can occur in the RV plumbing system due to wear and tear or improper installation. They can cause water damage to the RV's interior and can also lead to mold and mildew growth.

Clogs: Clogs can occur in the RV's pipes, especially if the RV is not properly maintained or if the wrong type of toilet paper or other materials are flushed down the toilet.

Water pressure issues: Water pressure issues can occur if the RV's water pump is not functioning correctly or if there is a blockage in the pipes.

Frozen pipes: In cold weather, RV plumbing systems can be susceptible to frozen pipes, which can cause the pipes to burst and result in costly repairs.

Tank sensor problems: Tank sensors can malfunction and fail to accurately report the levels of waste or freshwater in the RV's tanks.

Water heater problems: The RV's water heater may fail to heat water or may produce insufficient hot water due to issues with the heating element or other components.

It is essential to perform regular inspection and maintenance of the RV plumbing system to prevent these problems and ensure that the system is functioning correctly. Issues or damage caused by improperly maintained plumbing systems is often not covered by the manufacturer's warranty.

Step-by-Step Guide for Troubleshooting the Water System in an RV:

Check the water supply: First, ensure that the RV is properly connected to a water supply and that the supply is turned on. If there is no water coming into the RV, there may be an issue with the water source, such as a broken hose, or a closed valve.

Check the water pump: If the RV is not connected to an external water source, check the water pump to ensure that it is functioning correctly. Listen for any unusual sounds, such as grinding or clicking, which may indicate a problem with the pump.

Check for leaks: Inspect the water lines for any leaks or signs of water damage. Leaks can occur in the water lines due to wear and tear, improper installation, or freezing temperatures. If a leak is detected, repair or replace the damaged section of the water line.

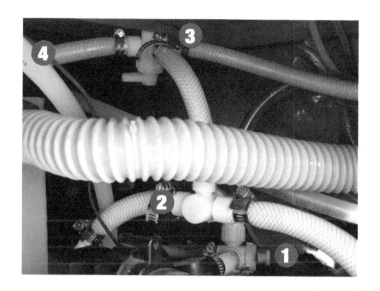

Check the water pressure: If the water pressure is low, there may be a blockage in the water lines or a problem with the water pump. Check the water filter for any debris or clogs, and clean or replace the filter if necessary.

Check the water heater: If the hot water is not working, there may be a problem with the water heater. Check the water heater for any leaks or signs of damage and ensure that the heater is properly connected and functioning correctly.

Regular inspection and maintenance of the RV's plumbing system can help prevent issues from arising. Check the water lines, water pump, water heater, and tank sensors regularly to ensure that they are functioning correctly and to identify any potential problems before they become more significant issues.

Troubleshooting an RV Water Pump

Here are some steps to troubleshoot an RV water pump:

Check the power source: Make sure the RV's battery is charged or the RV is plugged in to a power source.   Check the circuit breaker and fuses to ensure they are not tripped or blown.

Check the pump switch: If the pump has power but isn't working, check the pump switch. Make sure it is in the "on" position.

Check for air in the lines: Air in the water lines can prevent the pump from working.   Turn off the pump and open a faucet. Let the water run until all the air is out of the lines. Then turn the pump back on.

Check the water level: Make sure there is water in the RV's freshwater tank. If the tank is empty, the water pump won't work.

Check the pump's filter: The water pump may have a filter that needs to be cleaned or replaced. Remove the filter and inspect it for debris or clogs. Clean or replace the filter as necessary.

Check the RV water filter (if installed): A clogged water filter can reduce the pump's flow rate or stop it from working altogether. Remove the filter and clean or replace it.

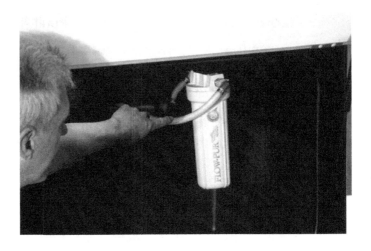

Check for leaks: Inspect the RV's plumbing for leaks or damage. Leaks can prevent the water pump from functioning properly.

Inspect the pump: Inspect the water pump itself for damage or wear. Look for cracks, leaks, or other signs of damage. Check the pump's connections to ensure they are secure. Check the pressure switch that regulates the water pressure to ensure that it is functioning properly.

Bypass Valve   Pressure Switch

By following these troubleshooting steps, RV owners can diagnose and fix many common issues with their water pump. If these steps don't solve the problem, it may be necessary to seek professional help from a qualified RV technician.

RV Holding Tank Issues

There are several common problems that RV owners may experience with their holding tanks. One of the most common problems with RV holding tanks is unpleasant odors that can develop over time. This can be caused by a buildup of waste and bacteria in the tank, or by leaks in the tank or plumbing system. Another common issue is clogging of the holding tank drain system. This can be caused by a variety of factors, including flushing non-degradable items down the toilet or sink, insufficient water usage, or a buildup of solids in the tank.

Holding tanks vibrate and flex when RVs travel down the road and can develop leaks over time. This can result in fresh or wastewater leaking out of the tank and causing damage to the RV.

Leaks can be caused by cracks in the tank, damage to the plumbing system, or improper installation of the tank. Also, the sensors that monitor the level of water or waste in the holding tank can sometimes malfunction, leading to inaccurate readings and difficulty in determining when the tank is full or needs to be emptied.

Regular maintenance of the holding tanks is essential to prevent many of these common problems. Neglecting to properly clean and maintain holding tanks can lead to expensive repairs due to buildup of waste, odors, and clogs. It is important for RV owners to be aware of these common problems and take steps to prevent and address them as needed to ensure that their RV's holding tanks operate efficiently and effectively.

Troubleshooting Holding Tank Issues

Step-by-step process for troubleshooting RV holding tank sensors:

If the holding tank sensor is indicating that one of your holding tanks is full, but you know it is not, the problem may be with the sensor itself. However, before assuming that the sensor is faulty, it is important to verify that the problem is not due to tissue paper being stuck on the sensor, a clog or other issue in the plumbing system.

Check the wiring: Make sure that the wiring for the holding tank sensors is properly connected and not damaged. Loose or damaged wiring can cause the sensor to malfunction.

Clean the sensors: The sensors may become coated with waste or debris over time, which can interfere with their ability to accurately detect the level of waste in the tank. Use a specialized holding tank sensor cleaner to remove any buildup from the sensors. There are many good brands available at retailers such as Walmart, Home Depot, Lowes, etc.

Replace the sensors: If cleaning the sensors does not solve the problem, the sensors may need to be replaced. This will require removing the old sensors and installing new ones in their place. Make sure to use sensors that are designed for your RV's specific make and model.

Consider a new monitoring system: It is generally known throughout the RV industry that holding tank sensors are rarely accurate. If the holding tank sensors continue to malfunction even after cleaning or replacement, it may be time to consider a new monitoring system.

There are several aftermarket monitoring systems available that use different technologies to measure the level of waste in the tank, such as ultrasonic sensors or pressure sensors.

It is important to note that troubleshooting holding tank sensors can be challenging, and in some cases, it may be best to consult a qualified RV technician to ensure that the problem is properly diagnosed and addressed.

Common Holding Tank Dump Valve Issues

There are several common problems that RV owners may experience with their holding tank dump valves. Holding tank dump valves can develop leaks over time, which can result in wastewater leaking out of the valve and causing damage to the RV. Leaks can be caused by cracks in the valve or damage to the plumbing system. Dump valves can become stuck or difficult to operate over time. This can be caused by a variety of factors, including debris or waste buildup, insufficient lubrication, or damage to the valve or handle. The valve handle that opens and closes the dump valve can sometimes become loose, detached, or difficult to turn or pull. This can make it difficult to operate the valve and can result in damage to the pull handle and waste not draining from the tank.

Some RVs use a cable-operated valve system, and the cables can sometimes become loose or disconnected. This can cause the valve to not operate properly, resulting in waste not draining from the tank. The rubber seals around the dump valve can become worn or damaged over time, which can cause leaks and difficulty in operating the valve.

It is important for RV owners to be aware of these common problems and take steps to prevent and address them as needed to ensure that their RV's holding tank dump valves operate efficiently and effectively. Regular maintenance and cleaning of the valves can help prevent many of these issues, as well as prompt repairs when necessary.

Step-by-Step Process for Troubleshooting RV Holding Tank Dump Valves:

Verify the problem: If the holding tank dump valve is not working properly, the first step is to verify the problem. This may involve testing the valve to see if it opens and closes properly, or checking to see if there are any leaks or other issues. If the valve appears to be stuck or not opening and closing smoothly, inspect the valve for any visible damage or debris that may be causing the problem. Look for any cracks, breaks, or obstructions that may be preventing the valve from functioning properly.

Cracked Black Tank Valve

Lubricate the valve: Dump valves may become stiff or difficult to operate over time. Lubricating the valve with a silicone-based lubricant can help to improve its function and prevent future problems.

Clean the valve: Dump valves can become clogged with debris, waste, or other material over time. To clean the valve, use a specialized holding tank valve cleaner or a mixture of warm water and dish soap to flush out any buildup or obstructions.

Replace the valve: If the valve is damaged or cannot be repaired through cleaning or lubrication, it may need to be replaced. This will require removing the old valve and installing a new one in its place. Make sure to use a valve that is designed for your RV's specific make and model.

Check the plumbing system: If the valve is functioning properly but waste is not draining from the tank, check the plumbing system for any clogs or obstructions. This may involve using a type of sewer snake or other tool to remove any blockages in the pipes.

It is important to note that the plumbing from the tank to the dump valves can be complex and difficult to troubleshoot, and in some cases, it may be best to consult a qualified RV technician to ensure that the problem is properly diagnosed and addressed.

COMMON PROPANE SYSTEM ISSUES

There are several common problems that can occur with RV propane systems. One of the most serious problems that can occur with an RV propane system is a gas leak. Gas leaks can be caused by a number of factors, such as damaged or improperly installed propane lines or defective fittings, loose connections, or a faulty regulator. The regulator is responsible for reducing the pressure of the propane gas as it flows from the propane tank to the appliances in the RV. If the regulator is malfunctioning or not installed properly, it can cause a number of problems, including poor gas flow, low pressure, and problems with the appliances.

Propane lines can also become clogged or dirty over time which can lead to reduced gas flow and problems with the appliances. Propane fired appliances, such as stoves, ovens, and water heaters, can also develop problems over time. These can include issues such as ignition problems, malfunctioning thermostats, and burner problems.

Problems with the propane cylinder or ASME tank itself can also occur, such as damage to the tank or the valve, or issues with the tank's pressure relief valve. It is important to have regular maintenance and inspection of your RV propane system to ensure it is functioning properly and safely. The propane cylinders on most towable RV are regulated by the Department of Transportation. The cylinders must be inspected and re-certified after ten years from the date stamped on the collar.

After the initial ten-year certification, the cylinders must be inspected and re-certified every five years. If you suspect any issues with your propane system, it is best to have it inspected and repaired by a certified technician.

Troubleshooting Propane Appliance Issues

Absorption Refrigerators

Many RVs have dual powered (electric/absorption) refrigerators. These refrigerators use propane to cool the unit when not connected to shore power or a generator.

Troubleshooting RV absorption refrigerators can be a complex process, but here are some general steps to follow:

Check for power: Make sure the refrigerator is receiving power from the RV's electrical system or from the propane system, depending on the type of refrigerator you have.

Check the thermostat: Ensure that the thermostat is set to the correct temperature and that it is functioning properly. If the thermostat is faulty, it may need to be replaced.

Check for blockages: If the refrigerator is not cooling properly, check for blockages in the ventilation system, such as dust or debris in the vent or condenser coils.

Check the burner assembly: For propane-powered refrigerators, check the burner assembly for obstructions or damage. Make sure the gas supply is adequate and that the igniter is working properly.

Check the cooling unit: If the refrigerator is still not cooling properly, the cooling unit may be the issue. Check for leaks or damage to the cooling unit and verify that the ammonia solution is circulating properly. If the cooling unit is damaged or malfunctioning, it may need to be replaced.

Check the door seal: Make sure the door seal is tight and free of damage. A faulty door seal can allow warm air to enter the refrigerator, reducing its cooling efficiency.

Consult the owner's manual: Consult the owner's manual for specific troubleshooting steps and recommended solutions for your particular model of RV absorption refrigerator.

Propane Stoves

Here are some general steps to follow for troubleshooting RV propane ranges:

Check the propane supply: Make sure that the propane tank is properly connected and that there is adequate propane in the tank. If the propane supply is low or not flowing properly, the range may not light or may not burn at the correct temperature.

Check the burner assembly: Inspect the burner assembly for any obstructions, such as food debris or dirt. Clean the burner assembly if necessary.

Check the igniter: If the range is not lighting properly, check the igniter. Make sure that the igniter is properly aligned with the burner and that it is clean and free of dirt or debris. If the igniter is damaged or not working, it may need to be replaced.

Check the gas pressure: Verify that the gas pressure is correct. If the gas pressure is too low, the range may not light or may not burn at the correct temperature.

Check the gas valve: Inspect the gas valve to ensure that it is functioning properly. If the gas valve is not opening or closing properly, it may need to be replaced.

Check the oven temperature sensor: If the oven is not heating properly, check the temperature sensor. Make sure that the sensor is properly connected and functioning correctly. If the temperature sensor is faulty, it may need to be replaced.

Additionally, consult your owner's manual for specific troubleshooting steps and recommended solutions for your particular model of RV propane range. As with troubleshooting other systems, if you are not comfortable troubleshooting your RVs propane appliances yourself, it is recommended that you have it inspected and repaired by a certified technician.

ROOFTOP AIR CONDITIONER ISSUES

Some common problems with RV rooftop AC units include:

Refrigerant leaks: Refrigerant leaks can occur in the AC unit due to normal wear and tear, improper installation, or damage to the unit. Leaks can cause the AC unit to malfunction and can also lead to the release of harmful chemicals into the environment.

Clogged filters: Air filters in the AC unit can become clogged with dust, dirt, and debris, which can reduce the efficiency of the unit and cause it to work harder, leading to increased wear and tear.

Faulty thermostats: If the thermostat in the AC unit is faulty, it may not accurately control the temperature or turn the unit on and off as intended.

Fan motor problems: The fan motor in the AC unit may malfunction, leading to reduced airflow and decreased cooling performance.

Electrical issues: Wiring problems or electrical component failure can cause the AC unit to stop working or produce only warm air.

Compressor problems: The compressor in the AC unit can malfunction, causing the unit to produce only warm air or fail to turn on at all.

Condenser coil issues: The condenser coil can become dirty or damaged, leading to reduced cooling performance and increased energy consumption.

It is important to perform regular maintenance and inspection of the RV rooftop AC unit to prevent these problems and ensure that the unit is functioning correctly. This can include cleaning or replacing air filters, checking and maintaining the refrigerant levels, inspecting and cleaning the condenser coil, and ensuring that the thermostat and fan motor are functioning correctly. If any significant problems are detected, it is recommended to consult a professional RV technician or air conditioning specialist for further assistance.

Step-by-Step Troubleshooting for Rooftop ACs

Troubleshooting an RV air conditioner can be a bit tricky, but with some basic knowledge and the right tools, you can diagnose and fix many common problems. One of the most common issues with RV air conditioners is a faulty capacitor. Here's how you can troubleshoot an RV air conditioner and replace the capacitor:

Step 1: Turn off the power.

Before working on any electrical appliance, including an RV air conditioner, make sure to turn off the power supply. This can be done by unplugging the unit or turning off the circuit breaker that supplies power to the air conditioner.

Step 2: Check the thermostat.

If the air conditioner is not turning on, check the thermostat to make sure it is set to cool, and the temperature is below the current room temperature.

Step 3: Check the air filter.

A dirty air filter can reduce the efficiency of an RV air conditioner and cause it to work harder than it should.

Remove the filter and clean or replace it if necessary.

Step 4: Check the condenser coils.

The condenser coils located on the outside of the RV can become clogged with dirt and debris over time, reducing the efficiency of the air conditioner. Clean the coils with a soft brush or vacuum cleaner.

Step 5: Check the capacitor.

The capacitor is a small, cylindrical component located inside the RV air conditioner. It stores electrical energy and helps the motor start and run smoothly.

A faulty capacitor can cause the air conditioner to hum but not start. Use a multimeter to test the capacitor. If the reading is zero or very low, the capacitor needs to be replaced.

Step 6: Replace the capacitor.

To replace the capacitor, turn off the power supply and remove the cover of the RV air conditioner. Locate the capacitor and carefully remove the wires attached to it. Make a note of which wire goes where.

Take the capacitor to an RV parts store and purchase a new one with the same specifications. Install the new capacitor by attaching the wires to the correct terminals. Replace the cover of the air conditioner and turn on the power supply.

It might seem a daunting task, but troubleshooting an RV air conditioner and replacing the capacitor can be done with some basic knowledge and the right tools. If you're unsure about any step or you're not comfortable working with electrical appliances, it's best to call a professional for assistance.

COMMON FURNACE ISSUES

There are several common causes of RV furnace issues, including:

Power supply issues: One of the most common causes of RV furnace issues is a lack of adequate power supply. Low voltage or a weak battery can cause the furnace to malfunction.

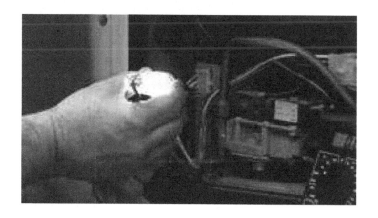

Dirty or clogged furnace filter: A dirty or clogged furnace filter can cause the furnace to overheat and shut down. It is important to regularly clean or replace the furnace filter.

Blockage or obstruction in furnace vents: Obstruction in furnace vents such as debris, mud dauber nests, leaves, or insects can cause furnace malfunction.

An RV furnace with a critter's nest inside

Faulty thermostat: A faulty thermostat can cause the furnace to stop working or function incorrectly.

Malfunctioning furnace igniter: A malfunctioning furnace igniter can prevent the furnace from igniting and producing heat.

Faulty blower motor: A faulty blower motor can cause the furnace to stop working or blow cold air.

Issues with the furnace circuit board: If the furnace is not working properly, the circuit board may be faulty.

Propane issues: A lack of propane or issues with the propane system can cause the furnace to malfunction or not work at all.

Wear and tear: Over time, the components of an RV furnace can become worn or damaged, leading to malfunctions or failure.

It is important to regularly maintain and service your RV furnace to prevent issues from arising. If you are unable to diagnose or fix the problem, it may be necessary to take your RV service center for repairs. Not all mobile RV technicians are certified to open and repair propane systems.

Troubleshooting Common RV Furnace Issues

An RV furnace is an essential appliance that provides warmth and comfort during cold weather. However, like any other appliance, it can develop issues over time. Here are some steps to troubleshoot common RV furnace issues:

Check the power supply: Make sure your RV has adequate power supply, whether it is coming from a generator or an electrical outlet. Low voltage or a weak battery can cause the furnace to malfunction.

Check the thermostat: Check the thermostat settings to ensure it is set to the desired temperature and in the correct mode (heat, cool, or fan). Make sure the batteries in the thermostat are fresh and properly installed.

Inspect the furnace vents: Check the furnace vents for any signs of blockage or obstruction. Make sure they are clean and free of debris, such as leaves or insects.

Check the furnace igniter: If the furnace is not igniting, check the igniter for any signs of damage or wear. If the igniter is not functioning properly, it may need to be adjusted or replaced.

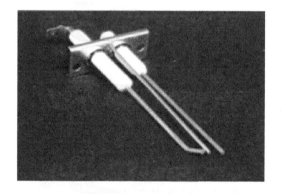

Check the furnace blower motor: A faulty blower motor can cause the furnace to stop working or blow cold air. Check the blower motor for any signs of damage or wear. Check the "sail switch" in the blower housing and make sure it is clear of obstructions. If it is not functioning properly, it may need to be replaced.

Check the furnace circuit board: If the furnace is not working properly, the circuit board may be faulty. Check the circuit board for any signs of damage or wear. If it is not functioning properly, it may need to be replaced.

If you are unable to diagnose or fix the problem, it may be necessary to take your RV to a professional mechanic or RV service center for repairs. Remember to always prioritize safety when troubleshooting and diagnosing RV furnace issues.

RV AWNING ISSUES

RV awnings can be a great feature that provides shade and protection from the elements. Awnings are relatively maintenance free if properly taken care of. This chapter addresses some of the basic issues RV owners encounter with awnings. Here are some steps to troubleshoot and diagnose RV awning problems:

Check the power supply: Check that your RV has adequate power supply, whether it is coming from a generator or an electrical outlet. Awning motors require a lot of power, and low voltage can cause problems with operation.

Inspect the awning fabric: Inspect the awning fabric for any signs of damage or wear. Look for tears, holes, or other damage that may be preventing the awning from extending or retracting properly.

Check the awning motor and gearbox: Check the awning motor and gearbox for any signs of damage or wear.

If you notice any grinding, clicking, or other unusual noises coming from the motor or gearbox, this may indicate a problem.

Look for obstructions: Look for any obstructions in the awning mechanism or the area where the awning moves, such as debris or objects that may have fallen in the way.

Check the awning arms: Check the awning arms for any signs of damage or wear. Make sure the arms are properly attached to the RV and are not bent or damaged.

Check the awning control system: If your RV has an electronic control system for the awning, check that it is functioning properly. A faulty controller can cause problems with awning operation.

Check the awning springs: Check the awning springs for any signs of damage or wear. Springs that are worn out or broken can cause problems with extending or retracting the awning.

If you are unable to diagnose or fix the problem, it may be necessary to take your RV to a professional mechanic or RV service center for repairs. Remember to always prioritize safety when troubleshooting and diagnosing RV awning problems.

Replacing Your Awning Material

Replacing the awning material on your RV can be a great way to extend the life of your awning and keep it looking new. Here are the steps to replace your RV awning material:

Remove the old awning fabric: Begin by removing the old awning fabric from the roller tube and the awning arms.

To do this, release the tension on the awning by unlocking the awning arms and carefully roll up the fabric. Then, detach the fabric from the roller tube and the awning arms.

Measure the new awning fabric: Measure the length and width of the old awning fabric and add an additional 6 inches to the length. This will give you the dimensions for the new awning fabric.

Purchase the new awning fabric: Purchase the new awning fabric from a reputable RV parts supplier or manufacturer. Make sure the new fabric is the correct size and style for your RV awning.

Install the new awning fabric: To install the new awning fabric, attach the fabric to the roller tube and the awning arms. Start by attaching one end of the fabric to the roller tube, then slowly roll the awning fabric onto the tube, making sure it is straight and taut. Attach the other end of the fabric to the awning arms.

Secure the new awning fabric: Once the new fabric is in place, secure it to the awning arms using the existing hardware or new hardware if needed. Make sure the fabric is evenly tensioned on both sides of the awning.

Test the awning: Finally, test the awning by extending and retracting it a few times to make sure it is working properly.

Replacing the awning material on your RV can be a straightforward process, but if you are unsure or uncomfortable doing it yourself, it may be best to have it done by a professional RV service center.

SLIDEOUT ISSUES

RV slideouts can be a great feature that allows you to expand the living space in your RV. However, if they encounter problems, it can be frustrating.

Here are some steps to troubleshoot and diagnose RV slideout problems:

Check the power supply: Check that your RV has adequate power supply, whether it is coming from a generator or an electrical outlet. Slideouts require a lot of power, and low voltage can cause problems with operation.

Check the slideout motor and gearbox: Check the slideout motor and gearbox for any signs of damage or wear. If you notice any grinding, clicking, or other unusual noises coming from the motor or gearbox, this may indicate a problem. RV slideout motors are usually located in one of several areas, depending on the make and model of the RV. Some possible locations for RV slideout motors include:

Inside the RV: In some RVs, the slideout motor may be located inside the RV, typically above the slideout, or in a compartment or under a piece of furniture.

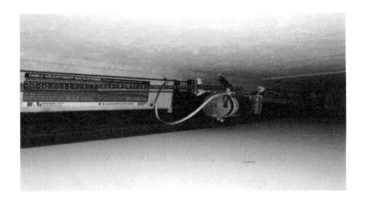

Under the RV: Some RVs have the slideout motor located underneath the RV, typically near the slideout mechanism.

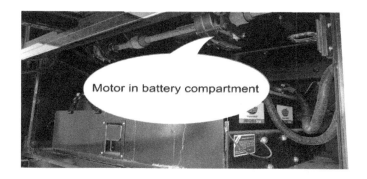

Motor in battery compartment

In the storage compartments: Some RVs may have the slideout motor located in one of the storage compartments, especially if the slideout is located near the rear of the RV.

In the exterior wall: In some RVs, the slideout motor may be located within the exterior wall of the RV, near the slideout mechanism.

It's important to consult your RV owner's manual to determine the exact location of your slideout motor. If you're unsure or unable to locate the motor, it may be best to consult with a professional RV technician.

Inspect the slideout mechanism: Inspect the slideout mechanism for any signs of damage or wear. Check the gears, rollers, and tracks to make sure they are in good condition and are properly lubricated.

Check the slideout controller: If your RV has an electronic controller for the slideout, check that it is functioning properly. A faulty controller can cause problems with slideout operation.

Look for obstructions: Look for any obstructions in the slideout mechanism or the area where the slideout moves, such as debris or objects that may have fallen in the way.

Check the slideout seal: Check the slideout seal for any damage or wear. A damaged seal can allow moisture or air to enter the RV, which can cause problems with comfort and energy efficiency.

Replacing a slideout seal on an RV generally involves the following steps:

Determine the type of seal you need: There are several types of slideout seals available, including bulb, wiper, and blade seals. You should purchase the same type of seal that is currently installed on your RV.

Remove the old seal: Use a putty knife or flathead screwdriver to gently pry the old seal away from the RV. Be careful not to damage the slideout or the surrounding area.

Clean the slideout: Once you have removed the old seal, use a clean cloth and a mild cleaning solution to wipe down the slideout and remove any dirt or debris.

Measure the new seal: Measure the length and width of the slideout where the seal will be installed. This will help you determine the length of seal you need to purchase.

Install the new seal: Starting at one end of the slideout, insert the new seal into the groove. Push the seal in as far as it will go, making sure it is properly seated. Continue working your way down the slideout until the entire length of the seal has been installed.

Test the seal: Once the new seal is installed, test it by closing the slideout and checking for gaps. If the seal is properly installed, it should create a tight seal between the slideout and the RV.

Replacing a slideout seal can be a bit challenging, so it's important to take your time and be patient. If you are unable to diagnose or fix the problem, it may be necessary to take your RV to an RV service center for repairs or have a qualified mobile RV technician evaluate it for repairs. Remember to always prioritize safety when troubleshooting and diagnosing RV slideout problems.

COMMON RV ROOF ISSUES

The single largest component and system on your RV is the roof system. One of the most common RV roof repairs is patching holes or tears in the roof material, which can occur due to branches, low-hanging obstacles, or general wear and tear caused by the natural flexing of the RV. Over time, the sealant used to seal the seams of an RV roof can deteriorate, allowing water to seep in. Leaks can occur in various areas of an RV roof, including around skylights, vents, and air conditioning units. Punctures to an RV roof can occur from a variety of sources, including tree branches, hail, or even foot traffic.

Regular cleaning and maintenance of an RV roof can prevent some types of damage and prolong its lifespan. This can include cleaning off debris and dirt, regularly inspecting the roof for signs of wear and tear, and applying protective coatings as needed. It is important to note that some RV roof repairs may require professional assistance, particularly if the damage is extensive or involves major components of the RV's roof system. Best practices also suggest that you should always let someone else know when you are going to be on the roof of your RV just in case of a fall.

Common Types of RV Roofing Materials

There are several types of RV roofing materials, each with its own advantages and disadvantages. The most common types of RV roofing materials include:

Rubber (EPDM): Ethylene Propylene Diene Monomer (EPDM) is a synthetic rubber material that is commonly used for RV roofing. It is lightweight, durable, and can withstand extreme weather conditions. EPDM roofs are relatively easy to repair and can last up to 20 years.

Fiberglass: Fiberglass is a popular RV roofing material due to its strength, durability, and resistance to damage from the sun and weather. It is lightweight and can be molded into various shapes, making it ideal for RVs with unique roof designs.

Aluminum: Aluminum is another popular RV roofing material due to its lightweight and durability. It is resistant to corrosion and can last for many years with proper maintenance. Aluminum roofing is also reflective, which can help keep the interior of the RV cooler in hot weather.

TPO: Thermoplastic Olefin (TPO) is a newer RV roofing material that is gaining popularity due to its durability and energy efficiency. TPO roofs are resistant to mold, mildew, and algae growth, and they reflect heat and UV rays, helping to keep the RV cooler in hot weather.

PVC: Polyvinyl Chloride (PVC) is a synthetic plastic material that is becoming increasingly popular for RV roofing due to its durability, resistance to weather and chemicals, and ease of maintenance. PVC roofs can last up to 20 years and are available in a range of colors.

It is important to note that the type of roofing material used on an RV can affect its weight, insulation, and cost, as well as the ease of maintenance and repair. Therefore, when making repairs it is essential to choose the right type of roofing material that meets your specific needs and budget.

Repairing Your RV's Roof

Repairing an RV roof can be a daunting task, but with the right tools and materials, it can generally be done by following these step-by-step instructions:

Materials needed:

Roof repair tape or sealant
Roof cleaner
Roof primer (if using sealant)
Roof coating (if using sealant)
Putty knife
Sandpaper or wire brush
Safety gear (gloves, eye protection, etc.)

Step 1: Clean the roof.

Start by cleaning the roof with a roof cleaner to remove any dirt, debris, or contaminants. Use a stiff-bristled brush to scrub the roof, paying extra attention to any areas that require repair. Rinse the roof thoroughly with a hose or pressure washer and let it dry completely.

Step 2: Inspect for damage.

Inspect the roof for any damage, such as holes, tears, or punctures. Mark any damaged areas with a piece of tape or marker so that you can easily locate them later.

Step 3: Prepare the repair area.

Using sandpaper or a wire brush, prepare the repair area by removing any loose or damaged material. The repair area should be clean, dry, and free of any debris.

Step 4: Apply the roof repair tape or sealant.

For smaller holes or tears, apply roof repair tape directly over the damaged area. Press the tape firmly in place, making sure it is fully adhered to the roof. For larger areas or more significant damage, apply roof sealant using a putty knife or caulking gun. If using sealant, apply a primer to the repair area first, following the manufacturer's instructions, and then apply the sealant in a thick, even layer.

Step 5: Let the repair dry.

Allow the roof repair tape or sealant to dry completely according to the manufacturer's instructions. This can take anywhere from a few hours to a day or more, depending on the type of repair material and the weather conditions.

Step 6: Apply a roof coating (optional).

If using sealant, apply a roof coating over the repaired area once it is fully dry. This will help to protect the repair from UV rays and extend its lifespan.

By following these steps, you can effectively repair an RV roof and prevent further damage or leaks. It is important to note that some RV roof repairs may require professional assistance, particularly if the damage is extensive or involves major components of the RV's roof system.

RV CABINETRY AND FURNITURE ISSUES

Some of the most common RV cabinetry and furniture problems includes the hardware that holds the cabinets and furniture in place becoming loose or damaged, causing the cabinets and furniture to shift or wobble. This is most often caused by vibrations during travel, and from regular use. Also, moisture can seep into the cabinetry and furniture, causing damage to the wood, veneer, or finish. This can be caused by leaks in the RV's plumbing system, condensation, or exposure to rain or other sources of water. Changes in temperature and humidity can also cause the wood used in RV cabinetry and furniture to warp or crack, as can exposure to heat, cold, or high humidity.

Regular use can cause wear and tear on RV cabinetry and furniture in the form of scratches, dents, and other damage that can detract from the appearance of the cabinetry and furniture. In some cases, poor craftsmanship during the manufacturing process can lead to problems with RV cabinetry and furniture after the RV is in service. Some of the more common issues include misaligned doors or drawers, uneven finishes, and other quality control issues. For this reason, it is important to regularly inspect the cabinetry and furniture in your RV to identify any issues and address them promptly. This can help prevent more serious problems from developing and extend the lifespan of your RV's cabinetry and furniture.

General Maintenance and Repair of RV Cabinets and Drawers

Here are some general steps to follow for troubleshooting and repairing RV cabinet and drawer problems:

First, examine the cabinet or drawer to identify the specific problem. Common problems include loose or damaged hardware, warping or cracking, wear and tear, or poor craftsmanship. If the problem is loose hardware, such as screws or hinges, tighten them with a screwdriver or drill. If the hardware is damaged, replace it with new hardware that is the same size and style.

Repair water damage: If the cabinet or drawer has been damaged by water, you will need to repair or replace the affected area. If the damage is minor, you may be able to sand and refinish the wood. If the damage is more severe, you may need to replace the affected area or the entire cabinet or drawer. Likewise, if the cabinet or drawer has warped or cracked, you may need to repair or replace the affected area. This may involve sanding, filling, and refinishing the wood, or replacing the entire cabinet or drawer.

If the problem is wear and tear, you may be able to repair the damage with wood filler or by sanding and refinishing the affected area. If the damage is more severe, you may need to replace the entire cabinet or drawer.

Address poor craftsmanship: If the problem is poor craftsmanship, you may need to make adjustments to the cabinet or drawer to improve its functionality or appearance. This may involve realigning doors or drawers, or adding additional support to the cabinet or drawer.

Remember, everything in an RV shakes and vibrates during travel. To prevent future problems, it is important to regularly inspect your RV's cabinetry and furniture and address any issues promptly. This can include tightening loose hardware, applying touch-up paint or finish, and keeping the cabinetry and furniture clean and dry. Also, these types of maintenance items are most often not covered by your manufacturer's warranty.

COMMON SUSPENSION AND RUNNING GEAR ISSUES

Some of the most common RV suspension problems involve worn out, misaligned, or damaged components. Over time, the various components of an RV's suspension system can wear out or get misaligned and become damaged. This can include springs, shocks, bushings, and other parts. If the tires on an RV are not properly aligned or balanced, it can cause uneven wear and tear on the suspension system, leading to problems such as uneven tire wear, vibrations, and handling issues. Overloading or uneven weight distribution in an RV can put additional stress on the suspension system, leading to problems such as sagging or uneven ride height.

Rough roads, potholes, and other road hazards can also cause damage to an RV's suspension system over time. Failure to properly maintain an RV's suspension system can lead to problems such as rust, corrosion, and worn out or damaged components. If you suspect that your RV has suspension problems, it is important to have it inspected and repaired by a certified technician as soon as possible. Driving an RV with suspension problems can be dangerous and can cause additional damage to the vehicle. Regular maintenance and inspections can help prevent suspension problems from developing in the first place.

Troubleshooting Wheel Bearing Issues

Wheel bearings are an essential part of any vehicle, including RVs. They support the weight of the vehicle and allow the wheels to rotate smoothly. If you suspect that your RV's wheel bearings are causing problems, here are some steps you can take to troubleshoot the issue:

Listen for noise: Wheel bearing problems can often be heard before they can be seen. If you hear a grinding or humming noise coming from your RV's wheels, it could be a sign of a wheel bearing problem. The noise may increase or decrease depending on the speed of the vehicle.

Check the temperature: After driving your RV for a while, touch the wheel hubs to check their temperature. If they are extremely hot, it could be a sign that the wheel bearings are overheating due to friction.

Check for play: With your RV parked, jack up the wheels and check for any play in the wheels by moving them back and forth. If there is a noticeable amount of play, it could be a sign of a worn or damaged wheel bearing.

Inspect the bearings: Remove the wheel and inspect the bearings for signs of wear or damage. Look for pitting or discoloration on the bearing races and rollers, which can indicate that they are worn. Also, check for any signs of damage or rust on the bearing itself.

Lubrication: If you notice that the bearings are dry or lack lubrication, it could cause premature wear and failure. Check to make sure that the bearings are properly greased and lubricated according to the manufacturer's specifications.

Replace the bearings: If you have determined that your RV's wheel bearings are worn or damaged, it's important to replace them as soon as possible. This will prevent further damage to the wheel and axle, and reduce the risk of a dangerous wheel failure while driving.

Reassemble: Once you have replaced the bearings, reassemble the wheel hub, making sure to torque the wheel bolts to the manufacturer's specifications.

Overall, it's important to keep your RV's wheel bearings properly maintained and lubricated to prevent premature wear and damage. Regular inspections and timely replacements can help you avoid expensive repairs and keep your RV running smoothly on the road.

Troubleshooting Uneven or Irregular Tire Wear

Uneven or irregular tire wear on an RV can be a sign of a number of different problems, including misalignment, improper tire pressure, suspension issues, or worn out parts. Here are some steps you can take to troubleshoot the issue:

Inspect the tires: Look for signs of uneven or irregular wear on the tires, such as feathering, cupping, or scalloping. Also, check the tire pressure and make sure that it's within the recommended range.

Check the alignment: Misaligned wheels can cause uneven tire wear. Use a straight edge or laser alignment tool to check the alignment of the wheels. Adjust the alignment as necessary according to the manufacturer's specifications.

Check the suspension: RVs have complex suspension systems that can contribute to uneven tire wear. Inspect the suspension components, including the shocks, struts, and springs, for signs of wear or damage. Replace any worn or damaged parts.

Check the wheel bearings: Worn or damaged wheel bearings can cause uneven tire wear. Inspect the bearings for signs of wear or damage and replace them if necessary.

Check the brakes: Worn or malfunctioning brakes can also cause uneven tire wear. Inspect the brake components, including the brake pads, rotors, and calipers, and replace any worn or damaged parts.

Rotate the tires: Rotating the tires can help to even out wear and extend their lifespan. Follow the manufacturer's recommendations for tire rotation intervals and patterns.

Balance the tires: Unbalanced tires can also cause uneven wear. Have the tires balanced by a professional.

Overall, it's important to address uneven or irregular tire wear on an RV as soon as possible to prevent further damage and ensure safe operation on the road. Regular maintenance and inspections can help you catch potential issues before they become major problems.

COMMON RV GENERATOR ISSUES

RV generators can experience a range of problems, but some of the most common ones include:

Fuel issues: One of the most common problems with RV generators is related to the fuel supply. Over time, the fuel can become stale and contaminated, leading to issues such as clogging of the fuel system and fuel lines, and dirty fuel filters. This can result in difficulty starting the generator or a generator that shuts off unexpectedly.

Battery problems: RV generators typically use a battery to start up, and if the battery is not maintained properly, it can fail to start the generator. Additionally, if the battery is not recharged properly, it can become depleted, leading to a generator that fails to start or one that shuts off unexpectedly.

Overheating: RV generators can overheat if they are not properly maintained or if they are overloaded. Overheating can cause serious damage to the generator and may require expensive repairs.

Carbon buildup: Carbon buildup on the generator's spark plug can lead to difficulty starting the generator or cause it to run rough. This can also cause damage to the generator's engine if left untreated.

Low oil pressure: RV generators require oil to lubricate their moving parts, and if the oil level is low or if the oil pressure is insufficient, the generator can suffer damage or fail to start.

To avoid these problems, it's important to follow the manufacturer's maintenance schedule and to regularly inspect and service your RV generator.

Troubleshooting Generator Issues

Here is a step-by-step guide to troubleshoot an RV generator that won't start or shuts down after only a few minutes:

Check the fuel level: For onboard generators, make sure that the RV has at least a quarter of a tank of gasoline or diesel. For portable units, just make sure the generator has enough fuel in the tank. If the fuel level is low, fill the tank with fresh gasoline.

Check the fuel filter: If the fuel filter is clogged, the generator won't be able to get enough fuel to run. Check the fuel filter and replace it if necessary.

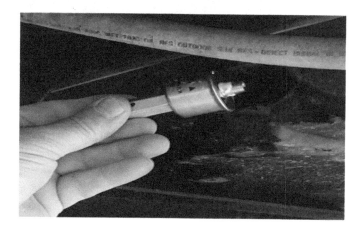

Check the oil level: Low oil levels can cause the generator to shut down automatically as a safety precaution. Check the oil level and add more oil if needed.

Check the battery: If the generator won't start, check the battery to ensure it has enough charge. If the battery is low or dead, try charging it or replacing it.

Check the spark plug (gasoline generators only): The spark plug may be fouled or damaged, which can cause the generator to run poorly or not start at all. Check the spark plug and replace it if necessary.

Check the air filter: A dirty or clogged air filter can restrict air flow and cause the generator to run poorly or shut down. Check the air filter and clean or replace it if needed.

Check the carburetor: A dirty or clogged carburetor can cause the generator to run poorly or not start at all. Check the carburetor and clean or rebuild it if necessary.

Check for overheating: If the generator runs for a few minutes and then shuts down, it may be overheating. Check for any obstructions blocking the air intake or exhaust, and make sure the generator is not overloaded.

Consult the owner's manual: If none of the above steps work, consult the owner's manual or contact a qualified technician for further assistance.

By following these troubleshooting steps, you should be able to identify and resolve most common issues that prevent an RV generator from starting or cause it to shut down after running for a short period of time.

RV LIFE SAFETY COMPONENT REQUIREMENTS

The life safety system in an RV typically includes a combination of components designed to protect the occupants from fire, smoke, and other hazards. Some of the key components that make up the life safety system in an RV include:

Smoke Detectors

Smoke detectors are an essential component of the life safety system in an RV, as they can help to alert occupants to the presence of smoke and potential fire hazards. Here are some of the important requirements for RV smoke detectors:

RV smoke detectors should be designed specifically for RV use and meet the requirements of the RV industry standards. It is recommended to use photoelectric smoke detectors, which are more sensitive to slow-burning fires and less prone to false alarms from cooking or shower steam.

Smoke detectors should be installed in key locations throughout the RV, including in sleeping areas, living areas, and near cooking appliances. They should be mounted on the ceiling and away from any vents or air conditioning ducts.

Smoke detectors in RVs should be hardwired to the RV's electrical system, and also have a backup power source such as a battery, in case of power outages. The batteries should be replaced annually or according to the manufacturer's recommendations.

Smoke detectors in an RV should be interconnected so that if one detector is triggered, all the detectors in the RV will sound an alarm. This can help to ensure that occupants are alerted to a potential fire hazard no matter where they are in the RV.

It is important to regularly test the smoke detectors in an RV to ensure they are functioning properly. The detectors should be tested at least once a month and the batteries should be replaced annually or according to the manufacturer's recommendations. In addition, smoke detectors should be replaced every 10 years.

Carbon Monoxide/LP Gas Detectors

Carbon monoxide (CO) and LP gas detectors are important components of the life safety system in an RV, as they can help to alert occupants to the presence of potentially deadly gases. Here are some important requirements for RV carbon monoxide and LP gas detectors:

RV carbon monoxide and LP gas detectors should be designed specifically for RV use and meet the requirements of the RV industry standards. It's recommended to use combination CO/LP gas detectors that can detect both carbon monoxide and propane gas leaks.

Carbon monoxide and LP gas detectors should be installed in key locations throughout the RV, including in sleeping areas, living areas, and near gas appliances. They should be mounted on the ceiling and away from any vents or air conditioning ducts.

Carbon monoxide and LP gas detectors in RVs should be hardwired to the RV's electrical system and have a backup power source such as a battery, in case of power outages. The batteries should be replaced annually or according to the manufacturer's recommendations.

Carbon monoxide and LP gas detectors in an RV should be interconnected so that if one detector is triggered, all the detectors in the RV will sound an alarm. This can help to ensure that occupants are alerted to a potential gas leak no matter where they are in the RV.

Testing and Maintenance: It is important to regularly test the carbon monoxide and LP gas detectors in an RV to ensure they are functioning properly. The detectors should be tested at least once a month, and batteries should be replaced annually or according to the manufacturer's recommendations. In addition, detectors should be replaced according to the manufacturer's recommendations, which is typically every 5-7 years for CO detectors and every 7-10 years for LP gas detectors.

Fire Extinguishers

Fire extinguishers are an important component of the life safety system in an RV, as they can be used to quickly extinguish small fires before they can spread and cause significant damage. Here are some important requirements for fire extinguishers in RVs:

Fire extinguishers used in RVs should be specifically designed for use in RVs and meet the requirements of the RV industry standards. It is recommended to use multipurpose extinguishers that are rated for Class 10 B, and C fires, which can extinguish fires involving ordinary combustibles, flammable liquids, and electrical equipment.

The size of the fire extinguisher needed for an RV depends on the size of the RV, but it should be at least a 5-pound extinguisher. It is important to make sure that the extinguisher is large enough to effectively extinguish a fire, but also small enough to be easily maneuvered in the tight spaces of an RV.

Fire extinguishers should be located in a visible and easily accessible location, within 24" of the entry door and in the kitchen area. They should be mounted in a bracket or holder to prevent them from moving around while the RV is in motion.

Fire extinguishers should be regularly inspected and maintained according to the manufacturer's recommendations. This includes checking the pressure gauge, making sure the pin and tamper seal are intact, and shaking the extinguisher to prevent the powder from settling.

It is equally important for all RV occupants to know how to use a fire extinguisher in case of a fire. Training should include knowing when to use an extinguisher, where the fire extinguisher is located, how to use it properly, and how to evacuate the RV safely in case of a fire.

Emergency Exits

RVs typically have multiple emergency exits, such as windows or doors, to allow the occupants to quickly escape in the event of a fire or other emergency. Emergency exits are a critical component of the life safety system in an RV. Here are some of the requirements for emergency exits in an RV:

RVs must have at least one emergency exit, but it's recommended to have multiple exits for added safety. The number of emergency exits required depends on the size of the RV and the number of occupants. Emergency exits should be located in the sleeping areas and living areas of the RV, and should be easily accessible.

Emergency exits in RVs should be large enough for occupants to escape through in case of an emergency. The minimum size requirement for emergency exits is 20 inches wide by 24 inches high, or 5 square feet of opening for each occupant.

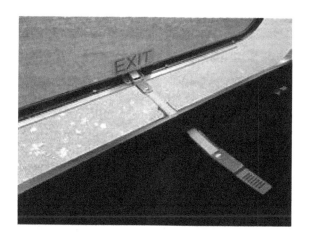

Emergency exits should be easily accessible and operable from both the inside and outside of the RV. They should be located no more than 44 inches above the floor, and should not require special tools or knowledge to operate.

Emergency exits should be equipped with latches or locks that are easy to operate, but that also prevent accidental opening during travel. The latches or locks should not require more than one motion to operate, and should be able to be opened without the use of a key or other tool.

Emergency exits should be clearly marked with signage or decals that indicate their location and operation, both inside and outside of the RV.

It is important to note that emergency exits should not be blocked or obstructed by any objects and should be regularly inspected and maintained to ensure they are functioning properly. In addition, occupants should be familiar with the location and operation of emergency exits in case of an emergency.

Please note that these components are not the only features that contribute to the safety of an RV. Regular maintenance and inspections are also critical to ensure that all systems and components are functioning properly and are up to date with current safety standards.

COMMON RV SPACE TERMINOLOGY

Every geographic region has its own subculture and its fair share of slang. The world of RV travel and camping is no different. While learning a new word in the wild can be a lot of fun, sometimes it's best to play it cool and prove you're in-the-know. So, I'd like to present 50 or so RV industry related terms to help you navigate conversations in the RV space like a seasoned pro. Here are 50+ common terms and definitions that will let you keep up with any road warrior or boondocker out there:

Airstream - a popular type of retro RV that looks like a repurposed aluminum aircraft fuselage.

Awning: A retractable cover used to shade the exterior of an RV.

Back-in Site - a site that needs to be backed into, the opposite of a pull-through site.

Batwing - the TV antenna of an RV, so named because of their alleged resemblance to a bat's wing.

Blackwater (tank) - dirty wastewater from toilets and the tank that holds it.

BLM – Bureau of Land Management, federal (public) lands available for short-term camping.

Boondocking - rugged, remote, and isolated RV camping, usually not in a campground and without hookups or amenities of any kind.

Bunkhouse - an area of an RV with bunk beds.

Camper - a generic RV term used by non-RVers to refer to all sorts of RVs.

Caravan - a travel trailer in the United Kingdom. Or a group of campers traveling in a group.

Class A Motorhome: A type of motorized RV built on a commercial truck or bus chassis, typically the largest and most luxurious.

Class B Motorhome: A type of motorized RV built on a van or panel truck chassis, often called a "camper van".

Class C Motorhome: A type of motorized RV built on a truck chassis with a cab-over bunk, typically smaller than a Class A but larger than a Class B.

Coach - an RV term for a class A motorhome (they look like a tour bus) or a high-end fifth wheel RV.

Curbside/Campside - the passenger's side of an RV.

Dicor – a commonly used roof sealant for RVs.

Diesel Pusher – a motorhome powered by a diesel engine located in the rear of the coach.

Dinghy - usually refers to a vehicle but anything towed behind an RV can be called a dinghy.

Dry Camping - anytime spent camping without hookups is called dry camping.

Dry Weight: The weight of an RV without any water or supplies.

Dump Station - a special area for offloading black and greywater from your RV's holding tanks.

Dually – a medium duty truck with 4 wheels on the rear axle used to haul larger towable RVs.

Fifth Wheel: A type of towable RV that is hitched to a truck bed using a fifth wheel hitch, typically larger and more spacious than a travel trailer.

Fiver - RV lingo for a fifth wheel.

Freshwater (tank) - drinkable water from your RV's sink and the tank that holds it.

Full Hookups - a campsite offering water, electric, and sewage connections.

Full-timer - someone who lives or travels in an RV exclusively.

Glamper - a person who loves glamping.

Glamping - a cross between glamorous and camping, staying at a campground with hook-ups and amenities.

Gooseball Hitch – a hitch ball in the center of a truck bed area for connecting gooseneck trailers (like horse trailers).

Gray water (tank) - dirty water from sinks and showers and the tank that holds it.

GVWR: Gross Vehicle Weight Rating, the maximum weight an RV can safely carry, including passengers, cargo, and fuel.

Holding Tanks - the name for the tanks holding black, grey, and freshwater.

Honey Wagon - a portable tank that campgrounds use to empty out waste from guest's RVs when they don't have sewer connections at each site.

KOA - Kampgrounds of America, a popular franchise of family-friendly campgrounds.

Leveling - making sure the RV is sitting level on all sides of a site.

Moochdocking - the act of parking in front of a friend's house or in their driveway, possibly siphoning their power for your RV.

Motorhome - any kind of RV that has its own engine and doesn't need to be towed.

NFS - National Forest Service, the administrators of the nation's 148 national forests.

NPS - National Park Service, the managers of all national parks, national monuments, and certain historical recreation areas.

Part-timer - people who live or travel in an RV for long stretches but also have a traditional home.

Pad - the name given to a parking spot for an RV on a campground (usually concrete).

PDI – Pre-delivery inspection.

Potable - drinkable water, safe to consume.

Pop-up Camper - a type of travel trailer made of canvas that pops open and unfolds into a camper.

Propane: A fuel used for heating, cooking, and other appliances in RVs.

Pull-through Site - a type of RV site that you can drive straight through, usually easier than a back-in for parking.

Rig - another generic term for all kinds of RVs, but commonly refers to large motorhomes and truck/towable combinations.

RV - a recreational vehicle. The umbrella term for any vehicle with living quarters whether it's a motorhome or travel trailer.

Shore Power - RV lingo adapted from the boating world, power from an external source.

Slide-out: A section of the RV that can extend outwards to increase living space when parked.

Snowbird - a person who travels to the south in an RV during the winter months to stay warm all year.

Sticks'n'bricks - a home, RVer term used to refer to a traditional house.

Teardrop Trailer - a kind of smaller travel trailer that has a teardrop shape.

Toad - another RVer term for something towed behind an RV.

Toy Hauler: A type of RV that includes a garage space for storing and transporting recreational equipment such as ATVs or motorcycles.

Travel Trailer: A type of towable RV that is hitched to a vehicle and can be unhitched when parked.

Truck Camper - a camper designed to slide into the bed of a pickup truck.

Wallydocking - Walmart is one of the few big chains that allow overnight parking. RVers refer to this as wallydocking.

Winnie - RV lingo for a Winnebago.

Workamping - exchanging labor for a camping or RV site and hookups, some RV parks may also include a small stipend.

WES - the three hookups RVers look for in campground accommodations: water, electric, sewer.

Now that you are familiar with the most common RV terminology, you're ready to hit the road!

NOTES FROM THE AUTHOR

I am not an academic. I am a seasoned Master craftsman who genuinely cares about the quality and safety of those who desire to explore the many benefits of RVing and the history and varied cultures of this great country of ours. My wife Trisha and I have spent most of our lives raising our children and seeing them become successful. Now our careers allow us the opportunity to work from our 43 ft fifth wheel RV office and see places we've only dreamed of or read about in other people's stories.

It is a dream of mine to have made a positive impact in someone's life before my time comes to an end. I sincerely thank you for purchasing this book and hope it saves you some of the headaches and frustration inherent in the RV lifestyle.

My Favorite Quotes:

"The significant problems we face cannot be solved by the same level of thinking that created them." – Albert Einstein

"The man person who will not read is no better off than the person who cannot read." – Mark Twain

"What will you paint on the canvas of your life, before you run out of space, or your paint dries up? - Trey Goudy, U.S. Congressman, SC

More books by this author:

RV Owners DIY Series (12 book series)

Available on Amazon

Made in the USA
Las Vegas, NV
23 December 2024

15297182R00069